Praise for other books by Michael W Lucas

SSH Mastery, 1st edition

"SSH Mastery is another must-have, must-read for anyone working in IT. I imagine that most of us use OpenSSH and/or PuTTY every day, but I am sure each of us will learn something about these tools and the SSH protocol after reading SSH Mastery." — *Richard Bejtlich, CSO, Mandiant, and TaoSecurity blogger*

"…one of those technical books that you wouldn't keep on your bookshelf. It's one of the books that will have its bindings bent, and many pages bookmarked sitting near the keyboard." — *Steven K Hicks, SKH:TEC*

"…SSH Mastery is a title that Unix users and system administrators like myself will want to keep within reach…" — *Peter Hansteen, author of The Book of PF*

"This stripping-down of the usual tech-book explanations gives it the immediacy of extended documentation on the Internet. Not the multipage how-to articles used as vehicles for advertising, but an in-depth presentation from someone who used OpenSSH to do a number of things, and paid attention while doing it." — *DragonFlyBSD Digest*

PAM Mastery

"Michael W Lucas nailed it." — *nixCraft*

"Fantastic." —*Kris Moore, BSDNow #171*

FreeBSD Mastery: ZFS

"Once again, a great FreeBSD book to read." — *Wendy Michele, nixCraft*

"ZFS Mastery covers what everyone using or administering these filesystems needs to know to work with them every day. It's fascinating to see how the system is used, having seen how it is implemented." — *George V. Neville-Neil, co-author of "Design and Implementation of the FreeBSD Operating System"*

Networking for Systems Administrators

"There is a lot of useful information packed into this book. I recommend it!" — *Sunday Morning Linux Review, episode 145*

After reading this book, you'll have a strong footing in networking. Lucas explains concepts in practical ways; he makes sure to teach tools in both Unix/Linux and Windows; and he gives you the terms you'll use to explain what you're seeing to the network folks. Along the way there's a lot of hard-won knowledge sprinkled throughout…" — *Slashdot*

FreeBSD Mastery: Specialty Filesystems

"a joy and treasure to read" — *Vivek Gite, nixCraft*

"I'm a fan of his books… he presents them in a way that makes them much more understandable. He has the right mix of humor and information." — *Sunday Morning Linux Review*

Sudo Mastery

"It's awesome, it's Lucas, it's sudo. Buy it now." — *Slashdot*

"Michael W Lucas has always been one of my favorite authors because he brings exceptional narrative to information that has the potential to be rather boring. Sudo Mastery is no exception." — *Chris Sanders, author of Practical Packet Analysis*

Absolute OpenBSD, 2nd Edition

"Michael Lucas has done it again." — *cryptednets.org*

"After 13 years of using OpenBSD, I learned something new and useful!" — *Peter Hessler, OpenBSD Journal*

"This is truly an excellent book. It's full of essential material on OpenBSD presented with a sense of humor and an obvious deep knowledge of how this OS works. If you're coming to this book from a Unix background of any kind, you're going to find what you need to quickly become fluent in OpenBSD – both how it works and how to manage it with expertise. I doubt that a better book on OpenBSD could be written." — *Sandra Henry-Stocker, ITWorld.com*

"It quickly becomes clear that Michael actually uses OpenBSD and is not a hired gun with a set word count to satisfy... In short, this is not a drive-by book and you will not find any hand waving." – *Michael Dexter, callfortesting.org*

DNSSEC Mastery

"When Michael descends on a topic and produces a book, you can expect the result to contain loads of useful information, presented along with humor and real-life anecdotes so you will want to explore the topic in depth on your own systems." — *Peter Hansteen, author of The Book of PF*

"Pick up this book if you want an easy way to dive into DNSSEC." — *psybermonkey.net*

Network Flow Analysis

"Combining a great writing style with lots of technical info, this book provides a learning experience that's both fun and interesting. Not too many technical books can claim that." — *;login: Magazine, October 2010*

"This book is worth its weight in gold, especially if you have to deal with a shoddy ISP who always blames things on your network." — *Utahcon.com*

"The book is a comparatively quick read and will come in handy when troubleshooting and analyzing network problems." — *Dr. Dobbs*

"Network Flow Analysis is a pick for any library strong in network administration and data management. It's the first to show system administrators how to assess, analyze and debut a network using flow analysis, and comes from one of the best technical writers in the networking and security environments." — *Midwest Book Review*

FreeBSD Mastery: Storage Essentials

"If you're a FreeBSD (or Linux, or Unix) sysadmin, then you need this book; it has a lot of hard-won knowledge, and will save your butt more than you'll be comfortable admitting. If you've read anything else by Lucas, you also know we need him writing more books. Do the right thing and buy this now." — *Slashdot*

"There's plenty of coverage of GEOM, GELI, GDBE, and the other technologies specific to FreeBSD. I for one did not know how GEOM worked, with its consumer/producer model – and I imagine it's complex to dive into when you've got a broken machine next to you. If you are administering FreeBSD systems, especially ones that deal with dedicated storage, you will find this useful." — *DragonFlyBSD Digest*

Absolute FreeBSD, 2nd Edition

"I am happy to say that Michael Lucas is probably the best system administration author I've read. I am amazed that he can communicate top-notch content with a sense of humor, while not offending the reader or sounding stupid. When was the last time you could physically feel yourself getting smarter while reading a book? If you are a beginning to average FreeBSD user, Absolute FreeBSD 2nd Ed (AF2E) will deliver that sensation in spades. Even more advanced users will find plenty to enjoy." — *Richard Bejtlich, CSO, MANDIANT, and TaoSecurity blogger*

"Master practitioner Lucas organizes features and functions to make sense in the development environment, and so provides aid and comfort to new users, novices, and those with significant experience alike." — *SciTech Book News*

"…reads well as the author has a very conversational tone, while giving you more than enough information on the topic at hand. He drops in jokes and honest truths, as if you were talking to him in a bar." — *Technology and Me Blog*

Cisco Routers for the Desperate, 2nd Edition

"If only Cisco Routers for the Desperate had been on my bookshelf a few years ago! It would have definitely saved me many hours of searching for configuration help on my Cisco routers." — *Blogcritics Magazine*

"For me, reading this book was like having one of the guys in my company who lives and breathes Cisco sitting down with me for a day and explaining everything I need to know to handle problems or issues likely to come my way. There may be many additional things I could potentially learn about my Cisco switches, but likely few I'm likely to encounter in my environment." — *IT World*

"This really ought to be the book inside every Cisco Router box for the very slim chance things go goofy and help is needed 'right now." — *MacCompanion*

Absolute OpenBSD

"My current favorite is Absolute OpenBSD: Unix for the Practical Paranoid by Michael W. Lucas from No Starch Press. Anyone should be able to read this book, download OpenBSD, and get it running as quickly as possible." — *Infoworld*

"I recommend Absolute OpenBSD to all programmers and administrators working with the OpenBSD operating system (OS), or considering it." — *UnixReview*

"Absolute OpenBSD by Michael Lucas is a broad and mostly gentle introduction into the world of the OpenBSD operating system. It is sufficiently complete and deep to give someone new to OpenBSD a solid footing for doing real work and the mental tools for further exploration... The potentially boring topic of systems administration is made very readable and even fun by the light tone that Lucas uses." — *Chris Palmer, President, San Francisco OpenBSD Users Group*

PGP & GPG

"...The World's first user-friendly book on email privacy...unless you're a cryptographer, or never use email, you should read this book." — *Len Sassaman, CodeCon Founder*

"An excellent book that shows the end-user in an easy to read and often entertaining style just about everything they need to know to effectively and properly use PGP and OpenPGP." — *Slashdot*

"PGP & GPG is another excellent book by Michael Lucas. I thoroughly enjoyed his other books due to their content and style. PGP & GPG continues in this fine tradition. If you are trying to learn how to use PGP or GPG, or at least want to ensure you are using them properly, read PGP & GPG." — *TaoSecurity*

Tarsnap Mastery

"This book is a great way to feel confident about backing up your data securely in cloud or through off-site backups, without compromising security or burning your pocket with enterprise grade products from IT vendors. If you use a Unix-like system I highly recommend Tarsnap service and "Tarsnap Mastery." — *Wendy Michele, nixCraft*

"If you use any nix-type system, and need offsite backups, then you need Tarsnap. If you want to use Tarsnap efficiently, you need Tarsnap Mastery." – *Sunday Morning Linux Review episode 148*

Relayd and Httpd Mastery

"Overall an excellent book which is typical Michael W Lucas' writing style. Easy to follow, clear cut instructions, and tons of new stuff to learn." — *Vivek Gite, nixCraft*

Ed Mastery

The Standard Unix
Text Editor

Michael W Lucas

Tilted
Windmill
Press

Ed Mastery

Michael W Lucas

Brief Contents

Complete Contents

Acknowledgements

My entire career—indeed, modern life for every one of us—would not have been possible without those giants who wrote entire operating systems using ed and its predecessors. We owe those giants a debt of gratitude.

More personally, though, I want to thank my technical reviewers who were kind enough to share their immense edpertise: Tim Chase, Josh Grosse, and Kurt Mosiejczuk. Any errors in this book crept in despite these fine folks' best efforts.

Many examples in this book were inspired by the fine presentations at the ed(1) Conference, available on Twitter at https://twitter.com/ed1conf and on Mastodon at https://bsd.network/@ed1conf. Attending the world's premier conference for text editing at 300 baud will help keep your ed skills razor-sharp.

After receiving rare but tediously ongoing complaints about my use of mixed male and female third-person pronouns in my technology books, I've prepared two editions of this book. Any third-person singular pronouns that appear in the standard edition, for normal people, are female. Those who believe that women don't belong in tech books are welcome to purchase the special "Manly McManface" edition, where all third-party singular pronouns are masculine. To compensate for this edition's much smaller market, though, the Manly edition is pricier than the standard edition. That's basic economics.

Also, one dollar of my proceeds from each sale of the Manly McManface Edition will be donated to my local chapter of Soroptimists International.

Chapter 0: Introduction

Let me be very clear here: ed(1) *is* the standard Unix text editor.

Dennis Ritchie, co-creator of Unix, declared it so. Who are you to argue with someone who can write a complete operating system without using a glass teletype?[1]

Many younger sysadmins naively hoist their pennants to defend overblown, overwrought, overdesigned text editors like ex, vi, or even the impossibly bloated nvi. A few are so lost as to devote themselves to turgid editors meant for mere users, such as vim and Emacs. This way lies not only appalling sysadmin skills, but an absence of moral fiber. As a sysadmin, you must have enough brain power to remember what you typed, to hold your own context in your head, and to truly commune with the machine on a deep and personal level.

Most Unix hosts exist to perform real work, such as supporting databases or serving web pages. When you specced out the system's memory, processor, and disk I/O, you considered the amount of hardware needed to run those tasks. Any system resources above that are intended to support atypical peak loads, not some pathetically overengineered text editor. When you suck up extra kilobytes—or, worse, megabytes—to run a fancy editor, you steal from the host.

Sysadmins dependent on something like vim? They actively harm systems. Do not trust them.

1	You know, a glass teletype. That toy that kids keep calling a "monitor," even though we all know monitors are reference speakers used in audio production.

For a random user, there's no shame in being unable to use ed. I'm not qualified to become a Navy SEAL. I'm not even qualified to become the kind of seal that lies on a beach and barks. That's okay. The world is full of computers. If you cannot handle the undiluted glory that is ed, use one of those friendly pointy-clicky systems. You're who they exist for. I recommend those tablet computers that don't have a keyboard, though, as those bright, colorful icons are very helpful to the non-*ed*ucatable.

It's not that using ed(1) is the pinnacle of systems administration achievement; it's the minimum requirement. You must be this competent to manage this computer.

If you're reading this book, it's because you want to join the elite. You want to count amongst the Navy SEALS of information technology. You want to be a real sysadmin, not one of those posers that need fancy toys like a "monitor." Yes, I own monitors, but only because these wimpy modern laptops don't come with built-in line printers.

Real sysadmins not only can work, they truly *thrive* on their wits and line printers alone. We welcome anyone who proves worthy of joining us.

This book covers standard ed. Many operating system developers can't resist the urge to add additional features to ed. That's how the tragedies of ex and vi happened, after all. While these developers' urge to become part of something as momentous as ed is perfectly understandable, ed is feature complete. This book won't cover OS-specific extensions, such as Linux's x and y commands and FreeBSD's encryption support.[2]

I should warn you, though: some sysadmins object to this book. They sincerely believe that the best sysadmins learn from studying

---

2 Why add encryption to ed? That's what crypt(1) is for.

the operating system source code or, at worst, reading the man page. Many of those folks forget their own youth, though. You can't learn computing on your own. Even the most sagacious Unix admins had mentors.

In this bleak age when search engine algorithms dredge up shoddily-assembled HOWTOs and pass them off as authoritative documents, providing for the next generation of sysadmins is one of the most vital tasks we face as a profession. I don't want the servers storing my retirement funds managed by so-called sysadmins who struggle against the pomposity of ex(1). Study the ed(1) source with this book at your side, in combination with a good C reference, such as the 1978 edition of "The C Programming Language" by the esteemed Brian Kernighan and Dennis Ritchie. If they could write a *complete operating system* using a line printer for output, you can handle your itty-bitty tasks.

Only a jerk would belittle you for attempting to transcend your limitations and become a proper sysadmin. Sadly, due to social stigma, I can't blame you if you hold owning this book a precious secret. If necessary, you can get instructions for making a protective book cover out of a brown paper bag from your nearest Gopher site.

Real sysadmins understand how the computer works. We understand that the long-sought "What You See Is What You Get" (WYSIWYG) editor is nothing but a pernicious lie from the marketing department. We know in our bones that a file ending in `.txt` isn't necessarily a text file—indeed, that a text file can have any name. Transcending these deceits is a necessary step to achieving true sysadmin mastery. The standard Unix editor does not pretend to be anything other than an engine for manipulating text.

And what a magnificent engine it is.

Chapter 1: Ed Essentials

At its heart, ed(1) is a text editor. It was written when computers didn't have monitors, though. Computers could write data to tape or to a printer. The printers of that day didn't wastefully run whole sheets of paper at a time, though; like ticker tape machines and typewriters, these *line printers* printed a single line at a time.

The sysadmin would enter commands, printing results only when necessary. Or, if you prefer, a clattering printer announced to everyone within hearing every time you lost your train of thought. Real sysadmins can concentrate on their work and remember context.

Ed is a line editor. It works on lines of text, as printed by a printer. It'll work perfectly well on one of those new-fangled "monitor" things, if you're unlucky enough to be stuck with one.

We'll begin exploring ed with a few basic tasks: starting the program, considering modes, saving, and quitting.

Starting Ed

Run ed(1) by entering ed and the name of the file you want to edit. Here I want to edit a text file containing my favorite poem, Lewis Carroll's *Jabberwocky*.

```
$ ed jabberwocky.poem
963
```

The number 963 does not appear anywhere within the poem. Why is it here?

When you edit a file, ed reads the whole file into a memory buffer. Like everything else in memory, the buffer disappears when the system

5

shuts down or the program exits. When you edit the file, you change the copy in the buffer. At some point you might overwrite the original file with the buffer, also known as "saving your changes." You could write the buffer to a different file, or a new file. When you start ed, it tells you how many bytes it read into the buffer. Remember, real software uses no more memory than necessary.

Where's the text? This is your file. Don't you already know what's in it? You don't really want to waste however many lines of paper auto-printing every file you open, do you? Next time try using head(1) to peek at the contents of your file before loading it into the editor, or flipping back through old printouts to identify the file.

Commands and Modes

Ed is command-driven, which is a fancy way of saying it's a text manipulation shell. You'll issue commands at the ed command prompt. Try it now by hitting ENTER.

```
?
```

Ed has one error message, a single question mark. It means "I don't understand you." When you get the error message, examine the command you typed and figure out what you did wrong. ENTER is not a valid ed command. All ed commands are letters, numbers, and standard keyboard symbols.[3]

The h command asks ed to explain the last error. With verbose error messages off, try ENTER again, then use h to explain the error.

```
?
h
invalid address
```

---

3   Ed is UTF-8 compliant, of course. While it can handle emoji, doing so imperils your immortal soul almost as much as using nano.

Everything's perfectly clear now, right? Probably not, but we'll discuss addresses in Chapter 10.

If you have an unlimited ink budget, you could enable verbose error messages. Enter H by itself to toggle verbose error messages on and off.

```
H
```

Ed echoes your command to the printer. Now try ENTER again.

```
?
invalid address
```

Turning on verbose error messages by default wastes both paper and reading time, but we've all had that experience where we stare at our command for far too long trying to figure out what we did wrong. We all need help to learn.

Another command you might find useful is turning the command prompt on and off. The ed command prompt is a single asterisk. It's useful when you're reviewing old printouts and need to identify your commands, or if you've got a fancy system with a video terminal. Enter P to turn the command prompt on or off.

```
P
```

If you're using a video terminal, you'll see the command prompt straight away. Printer users will get the command prompt in the line that displays their next command.

Enter ed commands individually. Some of those commands, such as for regular expressions (Chapter 101) can be very complicated and contain many characters, but each command needs its own line. Here I try to simultaneously turn on verbose error messages and the command prompt.

```
HP
?
```

I've confused ed. Let's get some detail.

```
h
invalid command suffix
```

Ed sees that I've used the H command and added the P suffix. An ed command suffix is much like a command-line argument; it modifies the command. The H command doesn't take P as a suffix, so ed spits an error in your face and declares you unworthy. Instead, enter each command separately.

```
$ ed jabberwocky.poem
963
H
P
*
```

You now have verbose errors and the command prompt. As you're just learning ed, many of the examples in this book are run with verbose errors and with the command prompt. It wastes ink, but you're worth it.

Leave ed with the q command.

```
*q
```

Set an alternate prompt when starting ed, using the -p flag.

```
# ed -p# jabberwocky.poem
```

You might need to quote your prompt, especially if you put a space between -p and your prompt. Prompts that have special meaning in the shell, such as * and >, will cause problems otherwise. For your own edification, try ed -p * jabberwocky.poem and see what happens. Otherwise, quote your prompt.

```
$ ed -p '>' jabberwocky.poem
963
>
```

All commands get run in command mode. Adding text requires input mode.

Switching Modes

While command mode is for issuing text editor commands, input mode lets you add text to a file. Here I open the empty file `todo`. It's an empty file, so it uses zero bytes.

```
$ ed todo
0
```

Ed supports three different ways to get into insert mode: append, insert before current line, and change current line. We'll discuss changing lines in Chapter 10.

Enter append mode with the `a` command. Append mode puts the cursor at a new line right after the current line. As this is an empty file, it goes straight to the end. Anything you type gets added to the file. Hit ENTER to go to the next line. Here I add today's to-do items to the end of this file.

```
*a
buy groceries
restrain capitalism
clean the rat cage
```

If I can accomplish all that, it'll be a good day.

Leave insert and append mode, returning to command mode, by entering a period on a line all by itself.

```
.
```

Insert text before the current line with the `i` command. This requires choosing a current line, which we'll discuss in Chapter 10. Similarly, you can choose an existing line and change it with the `c` command.

If you make a mistake in your command, CTRL-C aborts it and returns you to a command prompt.

I now have my to-do list in the buffer. Writing it to disk would be a good idea.

Saving and Exiting

Write the buffer back to the file with the w command. (We'll discuss saving to alternate files in Chapter 100). Ed prints the number of bytes written. After saving, exit ed with the q command. My complete ed session to create my to-do list would look like this.

```
$ ed todo
0
P
*a
buy groceries
restrain capitalism
clean the rat cage
.
*w
53
*q
```

While you can't normally combine commands, you *can* combine the write and quit command.

```
*wq
```

If your brain slips and you don't save the file before exiting, ed complains.

```
*q
?
```

Let's see what it's complaining about.

```
*h
warning: file modified
```

I didn't save the file. Enter the q command a second time to throw away your changes and exit without saving. You can also use a Q to immediately exit without saving.

Now let's consider line addressing.

Chapter 10: Addresses

In ed terms, an address is a line number in a buffer. Your commands affect an address. Many commands have effect on an address-by-address basis, such as "delete address" or "insert after address 5." Ed also has a concept of the current address, which is the default location. You can tell ed that you're working on line 5, and then change, append, or otherwise mangle that position in the file. Ed makes heavy use of addresses. Selecting and setting addresses is a vital part of working with ed.

We'll demonstrate addresses using a file containing Carroll's poem *Jabberwocky*. While I'm certain most of my readers, being decent and worthwhile people, are not only familiar with this poem but have it memorized, Appendix A includes a copy for those of you suffering from an appallingly deficient liberal arts education. It's thirty-four lines long, counting the blank lines between paragraphs, so it contains thirty-four possible addresses. A few ed commands (but not all) can accept an address of zero, meaning "before address one."

Many ed commands expect you to put the addresses to be affected before the command. A command like `4d` or `3,5c` means "on these lines, run this command." This swaps the most vital context out of your vulnerable brain and into the computer as quickly as possible. You know you need to delete lines, but your mind is most likely to forget the specific lines so it's best to set those immediately.

An address on its own is a single address. Two comma-separated addresses represent start and stop addresses, and include those addresses as well as everything between them.

11

When you set an address, ed prints the line. For clarity in this section, I set the P and H commands when starting ed.

Setting Your Address

When you first open a file, your current address is the last line of the file. Send the contents of the current address to your printer (or, if you're one of the fancy folks, to your monitor) with the p command.

```
*p
  And the mome raths outgrabe.
```

This is the last line of *Jabberwocky*. The special address $ always refers to the last line of a file.

To set the address to a line number, enter that number. I want to see line 6 of *Jabberwocky*.

```
*6
"Beware the Jabberwock, my son!
```

When you change the address, ed automatically prints the line at that address.

Advance the address one line at a time with the + command.

```
*+
  The jaws that bite, the claws that catch!
*+
Beware the Jubjub bird, and shun
*+
  The frumious Bandersnatch!"
```

To forward multiple lines, give the + command and the number of lines you want to forward. This is the last line of the stanza, and I want to skip the blank line that follows,[4] so I advance two.

```
*+2
He took his vorpal sword in hand;
```

---

4   Remembering that the file has blank lines is the sort of thing you must do if you wish to be worthy of ed(1).

Walk backwards through the buffer using the – or ^ commands. (GNU ed has disrespectuflly dropped the ^ command, leaving you with only –.) Add a number to move back that many lines.

```
*_
```

The previous line is blank—but we knew that. It's why we skipped ahead. Set the address back one more.

```
*_
  The frumious Bandersnatch!"
```

The Bandersnatch is, indeed, frumious.

Finding Your Address

The equal command (=) prints an address. It defaults to the last address of the buffer.

```
*=
34
```

This buffer is 34 lines long.

The period (.) represents the current address. To see your current address, enter a period and the equals sign.

```
*.=
9
```

Our address is 9, so we're on the ninth line of the file.

The address $ represents the last line of the file. While it's most commonly used to jump to the end, you can combine it with the equals command to explicitly list the number of lines in the file.

```
*$=
34
*$
```

I remembered correctly; this file is 34 lines long. And we've now moved to the end.

Address Ranges

Ed can perform operations on multiple lines simultaneously through two special addresses, the comma (,) and the semicolon (;).

The comma (also available as %) represents the whole file. It doesn't do anything by itself—you can't set the current address to "the whole file," but combined with another command you can perform actions on the whole file at once. Here I combine the comma with the p command to print the entire file.

```
*,p
'Twas brillig, and the slithy toves
  Did gyre and gimble in the wabe:
All mimsy were the borogoves,
  And the mome raths outgrabe.

"Beware the Jabberwock, my son!
  The jaws that bite, the claws that catch!
Beware the Jubjub bird, and shun
  The frumious Bandersnatch!"
...
```

Not only does this waste a lot of paper, everyone within hearing distance of your line printer will know that you're either too lazy to go through the earlier parts of the roll to find a copy, or you hate trees.

The semicolon represents the current address to the end of the file, just like ., $. Suppose you want to display the last nine lines of the file—two stanzas of the poem. The file is 34 lines long, so you want lines 26 through 34. Set the current address to 26 and send the rest of the file to the printer.

```
*26
"And hast thou slain the Jabberwock?
*;p
"And hast thou slain the Jabberwock?
  Come to my arms, my beamish boy!
O frabjous day! Callooh! Callay!"
  He chortled in his joy.
```

```
'Twas brillig, and the slithy toves
  Did gyre and gimble in the wabe:
All mimsy were the borogoves,
  And the mome raths outgrabe.
```

Yes, you see line 26 twice. You're clearly a tree-hater to print all this, though, so it furthers your goals.

If you change your address to a range of addresses, your current address becomes the last address of the range.

Relative Addresses

You can also access lines via relative addresses. A relative address is a certain number of lines before or after the current address, indicated by a plus (+) or minus (-) sign. There's lots of good reasons to do this.

*30

I set my address and ed shows me the contents—a blank line. Where exactly in the poem am I?

*-2,+2p
```
O frabjous day! Callooh! Callay!"
  He chortled in his joy.

'Twas brillig, and the slithy toves
  Did gyre and gimble in the wabe:
```

Ah, that's where.

Yes, I could do the same thing with a command like 28,32p. Relative addresses are just one of ed's many user-friendly conveniences.

A single minus or plus sign on its own means one. The command -p means "print the previous line," while -,+p gives one line of context on either side of the current address.

Scrolling

The scrolling feature is how ed condescends to assist those folks who insist on relying on a "monitor." The z command tells ed to scroll from the next address to as far as the terminal allows.

The standard terminal can display 24 lines at a time. Let's see how scrolling works. Start at the top of *Jabberwocky*.

```
*1
'Twas brillig, and the slithy toves
```

Ed prints the line at this address. Now scroll by running z.

```
*z
  Did gyre and gimble in the wabe:
All mimsy were the borogoves,
  And the mome raths outgrabe.
...
```

Ed starts with line two, because you've already seen line 1 and surely you can remember what you just read, right? The output continues until it fills the terminal, twenty-four lines later.

```
He left it dead, and with its head
  He went galumphing back.
*
```

Want to see more of the buffer? Hit z again.

To start scrolling at a particular line, put the address before z. Maybe you want the scroll to include line 1.

```
*1z
'Twas brillig, and the slithy toves
  Did gyre and gimble in the wabe:
...
```

To scroll a reduced number of lines, enter the number of lines you want to show after z. Here I scroll the third verse of *Jabberwocky*. Each verse is four lines long followed by a blank line. We want addresses 11 through 14, also known as 11 and the three addresses after 11.

```
*11z3
He took his vorpal sword in hand;
  Long time the manxome foe he sought--
So rested he by the Tumtum tree
  And stood awhile in thought.
```

Verse 3, suitable for framing!

The z command changes the current address to the last line shown.

Displaying Addresses

When you're working on a long file, it might make sense to print a convenient master copy of the file with the address of each line. The n command shows each line prefixed with its address. You can use n with selected lines by putting the desired start and stop address before the command, separated by a comma.

```
*11,14n
11      He took his vorpal sword in hand;
12          Long time the manxome foe he sought--
13      So rested he by the Tumtum tree
14          And stood awhile in thought.
```

Ed's current address becomes the last address shown, or 14 here.

Or you could print the entire file, conveniently numbered.

```
*,n
1       'Twas brillig, and the slithy toves
2           Did gyre and gimble in the wabe:
3       All mimsy were the borogoves,
4           And the mome raths outgrabe.
...
```

Only do this once you're done rearranging your files, or you'll waste paper.

Viewing Trailing Space

One annoyance with text files is that blank spaces can mess up a file. You'll notice extra blank spaces in the middle of your text, but those extra spaces at the end of a line are tricky. You don't want to have to watch your printer to see if the head carries way over to represent the blank spaces, after all. Use the 1 suffix after n or p to put a $ symbol at the end of each line. Here I view the actual spaces in the file containing my to-do list.

```
*,nl
1          have bath $
2          with soap$
```

There's an extraneous space at the end of line 1.

Bookmarks

Scrolling through a long file can be a pain, especially if you're adding and removing lines. Ed allows you to create bookmarks to easily return to a location in the file. Each bookmark is named after a single lower case letter, and you'll use that letter to return to the bookmark.

Suppose you want to place a bookmark at the beginning of each verse of *Jabberwocky*. You can't number bookmarks, but you can call each of the seven verses *a*, *b*, *c*, and so on, up to *g*. Use the k command to assign a bookmark.

```
*1
'Twas brillig, and the slithy toves
*ka
*6
"Beware the Jabberwock, my son!
*kb
...
```

Every five lines you'll create a new bookmark.

To return to a bookmark, use the single quote and the bookmark letter.

```
*'b
"Beware the Jabberwock, my son!
```

Now that you can dance through your files, let's mangle some buffers.

Chapter 11: Text Editing

Ed contains everything you need to change existing text files. As a simple example we'll muck with my to-do list. You can insert lines, join lines together, shuffle text around, and generally proceed with your day without worrying about all kinds of menus and knobs.

Changing Lines

A key function of a text editor is changing existing text. In ed this means selecting (by address) the line you want to edit, and changing it. Here's my to-do list.

```
*,p
buy groceries
restrain capitalism
clean the rat cage
```

Line two is not correct. I need to change it, and I need to add a new item between lines two and three. Set the address to line 2.

```
*2
restrain capitalism
```

Ed prints the address you set. Yes, that's the line I want. Go into insert mode with the change (c) command. Unlike plain insert, c overwrites the existing line.

```
*c
```

Type the new line two, hit ENTER, and add another line. Leave insert mode with a period on a line by itself.

```
obliterate capitalism
rainbow ponies all around
.
```

If I wasn't completely confident in my ed skills, I could double-check the buffer.

```
*,p
buy groceries
obliterate capitalism
rainbow ponies all around
clean the rat cage
```

Yes, that's right. I use the `wq` command to save my to-do list.

Inserting Amidst the File

The append (`a`) command adds a line after the current address. The insert before (`i`) command inserts a new line before the current address. Which should you use? Whatever does what you want to accomplish. I need to insert two new lines at the very beginning of the file, so I set the address to 1 and use the `i` command to put my new lines before that address. While I could give the `1` command and then `i`, it's simpler to give the address with the `i` command.

```
*1i
invest in guillotines
flee to private island
.
```

My to-do list now has six items.

Moving Text

I work down my to-do lists from top to bottom. This means ordering is important. Once my morning tea delivers consciousness to my brain, I'll realize that I can't very well purchase groceries after fleeing to the private island; I must take food *with* me. I'm pretty sure that I added "flee to private island" before "buy groceries," however.

```
*1,3n
1        invest in guillotines
2        flee to private island
3        buy groceries
```

Yep, I messed up. I should have added my new items after line 1, rather than inserting them before. Fortunately, ed offers the m (move) command.

The move command uses addresses both before and after the command. The addresses to be moved go before the command, on the left side. The lines get inserted after the address on the right side, after the m. You can use zero as the right side address, to put those lines at the top of the file.

```
*3m1
```

What was address 3 (buy groceries) should now appear after address 1 (invest in guillotines). Did I screw anything else up? I'll show the list with addresses, because I like numbers.

```
*,n
1       invest in guillotines
2       buy groceries
3       flee to private island
4       obliterate capitalism
5       rainbow ponies all around
6       clean the rat cage
```

No, hang on. I won't travel with dirty rats, but I must get groceries before cleaning the cage. Move line 6 to after line 2.

```
*6m2
*,n
1       invest in guillotines
2       buy groceries
3       clean the rat cage
4       flee to private island
5       obliterate capitalism
6       rainbow ponies all around
```

This still has problems. I know me. Investing, also known as "futzing around on this new-fangled Web contraption," is much more amusing than tedious chores. I really need to move items 2 and 3 to the top of the list. As that's before address 1, I use a destination address of 0.

```
*2,3m0
*,n
1       buy groceries
2       clean the rat cage
3       invest in guillotines
4       flee to private island
5       obliterate capitalism
6       rainbow ponies all around
```

Yes, much better.

When you move lines to after a later line, ed uses the current line numbers as of the time you run the command. Moving line one to after line twelve shifts all the lines up one, yes. What was line one becomes line twelve; it doesn't recursively start renumbering lines. Future move commands will use the new addresses.

When I use multiple move commands, I start from the end of the buffer to reduce the amount of math I do.

Deleting Lines

This is an ambitious list. Can I really get all of this done today?

Realistically, I know that once I start dinking around on the computer I probably won't get out of my comfy chair for the rest of the day. It's best that I get rid of any items that would let me relax in front of a printer. Use the d command to delete addresses. Here I delete line 3.

```
*3d
```

I could specify multiple lines by separating them with a comma, just as in moving lines.

The buffer now has a new line three, of course. When deleting multiple lines at different parts of the file, it's best to start at the end and work backwards. When you delete an address, the address of all later lines shifts up one. Working backwards reduces the amount of brainpower you waste on renumbering.

Undo

I'm as guilty of laziness as the next person. I need to develop the self-discipline to get up from the computer when I have stuff to do. That deleted item needs to go back on the list. Use the u command to undo your last action.

```
*u
```

Ed has one level of undo. It can only affect the very last command you ran, including undo. To redo, undo the undo. Hitting u three times undoes the undone undo. I can delete and re-insert this line forever, but undo will never go back as far as reversing my line rearrangements. That's more than one command back.

Regular expression operations (see Chapter 101) that affect multiple lines are a single command. You undo and redo such changes as a whole.

Inserting Text from Files

I perform certain tasks at the beginning of every day. For my convenience, I've created a separate file containing those items. The r command lets you read from another file. Here I read the file *usualtodo* and put it after address 0. That file gets added at the beginning of the buffer.

```
*0r usualtodo
21
```

21 bytes get read. What does my list look like now?

23

```
*,n
1        have bath
2        with soap
3        buy groceries
4        clean the rat cage
5        invest in guillotines
6        flee to private island
7        obliterate capitalism
8        rainbow ponies all around
```

Much better.

Joining Lines

Hang on, my list is messed up. The first two items should be one. Has some newbie playing with a bloated editor like ex(1) inserted a carriage return into my file? I'll execute the flunky responsible later, but for now, let's join those lines with the j command. The addresses you want to join get deleted from the buffer and replaced by a single line containing all their contents.

The j command uses addressing syntax similar to n. You might find it useful to double-check the line numbers you want to join before nailing them together. It's much easier to join lines than break them apart.

```
*1,2n
1        have bath
2        with soap
```

Yes, those are the correct lines. Merge them into one line and double-check the results.

```
*1,2j
*1,2n
1        have bath with soap
2        buy groceries
```

Much better. Ed's current address changes to that of the merged line—in this case, 1.

Note that the previous line one had a space at the end, as shown in Chapter 10. Without that space, the words would have run together. You'd have to change that line to fix the missing space.

Splitting lines requires using a substitution, discussed in Chapter 110.

Copying Lines

This is going to be a long day. I'm pretty sure I'll need a bath at the end of it. Worse, the pet rats will be indignant after being hauled off to a private island. Their cage will need cleaning. Rather than laboriously typing out those items at the end of the to-do list, though, I'll copy them using the t (transfer) command. Put the address (or range of addresses) you want to copy before the command, and the destination after. The t command leaves your address at the last line copied.

I just re-addressed the file by joining the first two lines, so I double-check the early addresses.

```
*1,3n
1       have bath with soap
2       buy groceries
3       clean the rat cage
```

Right. I need 1 and 3 copied to the bottom of the list. I want to go to bed properly clean, so I start by copying "clean the rat cage" (address 3) to the very end of the file.

```
*3t$
```

Now I can copy address 1 to the end of the file, putting my bath after cleaning.

```
*1t$
```

How did this come out?

```
*,n
1          have bath with soap
2          buy groceries
3          clean the rat cage
4          invest in guillotines
5          flee to private island
6          obliterate capitalism
7          rainbow ponies all around
8          clean the rat cage
9          have bath with soap
```

My to-do list is done. When I'm finished taking on the world, at least I'll be clean.

While I've copied addresses to the end of the buffer, you can put them anywhere. One interesting possibility is copying the line to right after the current address, using the period (.). This doubles the line, and leaves your address set at the second copy. You can perform transformations on that duplicated line while not touching the original, as we'll see in Chapter 110.

Appending Lines to Another File

Use the w command to append addresses in your buffer to another file. Put the lines you want to include before the command, and the name of the file to be added to at the end.

Nobody ever finishes everything on their to-do list. Here I copy what I didn't finish onto the end of tomorrow's list.

```
*5,9W tomorrow-todo
110
```

Here's hoping tomorrow is more productive.

Simple editing and rearranging suffices for a to-do list. But sometimes you'll want your text editor to interact with the operating system. We'll discuss that next.

Chapter 100: File Management and Shell Escapes

Opening an existing file is great, but what if you want to create a new file? Or maybe you're editing one file and want to switch to another? Perhaps you want to pull the output of a command into a file? Ed lets you do all this and more.

We'll start with file manipulations, and then proceed to commands.

The Empty Buffer

We've only started ed by editing an existing file. You can run ed without a file, though.

```
$ ed
H
P
*
```

Ed gives us an empty buffer. Let's fill this void.

```
*i
?
invalid address
```

What is it complaining about here?

Remember that the insert (i) command inserts a line before the current address. This is an empty buffer, so what is the current address? While you could make sensible guesses, ed will tell you if you ask.

27

```
* .=
0
```

Addresses are all positive. There's nothing in this file to insert a new entry in front *of*.

We can append, though. Let's create a couple lines of text.

```
*a
once upon a midnight dreary
while i pondered weak and weary
.
```

There's some text; now let's save it to a file.

```
*w
?
no current filename
```

What fresh inferno is this?

The Default Filename

Ed doesn't know what file you're working on unless you tell it. It doesn't blindly assume that you even want your buffer backed to a file at all; perhaps this buffer is security-sensitive and should remain entirely in memory. When you edit an existing file, ed assumes that you'll want to save any changes to that same file, but lets you write to a different file by changing the default filename.

The *default filename* is the name of the file ed writes the buffer to. Opening a file assigns the default filename to the name of the file, exactly as you'd expect. When you run ed without a filename, though, the default filename is blank. Use the f command to set the filename. Here I take my buffer of badly typed poetry, assign it a filename, and save it.

```
*f raven.poem
raven.poem
*wq
60
```

When I want to mistype more of this poem, I can open it by filename and save myself the trouble.

The w command can also set the default filename, if you give it one.

```
*w empty
0
```

The default filename lets you save your buffer with alternate filenames. Lesser text editors implement this as "Save As" functionality. Suppose I want to redo the way *Jabberwocky* is formatted. It's likely that I'll damage the text somehow, or wind up with something that looks worse than the original, so I want to work on a copy of the file. I change the default filename and save.

```
*f jabberwocky-hackedup.poem
jabberwocky-hackedup.poem
*w
963
```

I can now muck with my copy and not damage the original file.

Ed expects you know which files already exist on your system. If you use w to write to an existing file, it overwrites what's in that file. To add to the end of a file rather than overwrite its contents, use w.

Switching Files

Why should you leave ed to edit another file? Switch the file you're working on with the e (edit) command.

Suppose I've been mucking with the way *Jabberwocky* is formatted in an effort to make it more visually appealing, and need to add an item to my to-do list. Use the e command and the desired filename to switch files.

```
*e todo
?
warning: file modified
```

Ed is warning me that I've changed my original file and haven't saved my changes. I must either save my changes with w, or use e a second time in a row to say "yes, throw away my buffer and open the new file." Here I throw away my buffer.

```
*e todo
146
*a
fix Jabberwocky formatting
.
*w
173
```

A senior sysadmin intending to discard the modified buffer will use E to skip the confirmation step.

```
*E todo
146
```

My to-do list is now updated.

Saving Part of the Buffer

Maybe you want to save a chunk of your current file to a different file. You can do this by giving the write (w) command addresses and a filename.

I have my to-do list open. My file containing the template of my daily to-do items, that I normally put at the beginning of each day, is messed up. I want to send the first item on my to-do list to that file, overwriting the corrupted version with the corrected version. I give the addresses, the w command, and the name of the file.

```
*1w usualtodo
20
```

This writes address 1, the first line, to the file usualtodo. It's twenty bytes.

Or, suppose I'm editing *Jabberwocky*. I want to write verse two to its own file. Addresses six through nine contain verse two. I give that address range, the write command, and the filename.

```
*6,9w verse2.poem
139
```

I get the 139 bytes of verse two in the file *verse2.poem*.

Writing part of the buffer to a file does not change your current address.

Shell Escapes

You'll frequently need to grab information from the underlying operating system: an IP address, a file name, something. Leaving the editor to look up a detail, only to restart the editor and recover your current address, is not only annoying—it's inefficient. That's where shell escapes come in.

A *shell escape* runs a single command outside of the ed shell, displays the output, then returns you to editing. This displays the command output. Ed uses the exclamation point (!) to trigger a shell escape.

Suppose I'm writing the host's sysadmin documentation, and I need to know the current IP address. I don't want to see all the virtual interfaces, only em0. Get this information with ifconfig(8).[5]

```
*! ifconfig em0
em0: flags=8843<UP,BROADCAST,RUNNING,SIMPLEX,MULTICAST> mtu 1500
    lladdr 08:00:27:03:eb:10
    index 1 priority 0 llprio 3
    groups: egress
    media: Ethernet autoselect (1000baseT full-duplex)
    status: active
    inet 203.0.113.209 netmask 0xffffff00 broadcast 203.0.113.255
```

This host's IP address is 203.0.113.209. I can now reference that in my document.

Sometimes you want to repeat a shell escape. Ed remembers the last shell escape you ran, and can repeat it with the !! command.

---

5   Real Unix ships with ifconfig. And ed.

```
* !!
ifconfig em0
em0: flags=8843<UP,BROADCAST,RUNNING,SIMPLEX,MULTICAST> mtu 1500
...
```

It first repeats the command, in case you forgot.

Sometimes you'll want to read the output of a command into a file. The r command can read the output of a shell escape into your file, much as it lets you read another file into your buffer.

*r !ifconfig em0
```
267
```

It's read in 267 bytes. Check the contents of your file and you'll see the command output

*,n
```
1    em0: flags=8843<UP,BROADCAST,RUNNING,SIMPLEX,MULTICAST> mtu 1500
2        lladdr 08:00:27:03:eb:10
3        index 1 priority 0 llprio 3
...
```

Ed normally appends output from shell escapes to the end of the buffer. If you want to put that output elsewhere, give the address you want to insert after before the prompt. Suppose I have a file that contains two lines.

```
This is ifconfig
That was ifconfig
```

I want to insert my ifconfig output between them, or after address 1.

*1r !ifconfig em0
```
267
```

If you lack confidence, check the buffer.

*,p
```
This is ifconfig
em0: flags=8843<UP,BROADCAST,RUNNING,SIMPLEX,MULTICAST> mtu 1500
...
That was ifconfig
```

Yes, it's in the correct place.

Send to a Program

Reading from a shell escape is nice, but you can also send to a program's standard input. This lets you feed your buffer or parts thereof into other programs. Perhaps I need to count how many words are in the current file, so I can see if I met my daily word production target. Much as ed(1) is the standard text editor, wc(1) is the standard text counting tool. Write the buffer to a shell escape.

```
*w !wc
      34      166      963
963
```

This file has 34 lines, 166 words, and 963 characters. The last line is from ed, declaring how many bytes it wrote. It should match the number of characters reported by wc(1), of course.

166 words today? I better get writing!

Starting with an Escape

Perhaps the next file you need to create and edit needs to start with the output of a shell escape. You could save your work, exit ed, restart ed, and run your shell escape. That's perfectly legit, but it lacks elegance.

The e command lets you create a new buffer pre-populated with the output of a shell escape. This does not change the default filename, however. You'll want to follow up with setting a new file to save to, either by using f to set the filename or w and a filename to save the new buffer.

```
*e !ifconfig
1049
*f ifconfig-full.txt
ifconfig-full.txt
*w
1049
```

The first command executes the shell escape `ifconfig` and reads in the output. The second, `f`, sets the default filename to *ifconfig-full.txt*. Finally, `w` writes the file to its new filename.

If you don't want to use the `e` command, you can use a shell escape when starting ed. Complex commands will need quoting.

```
$ ed !'ifconfig em0'
```

You can now fold, spindle, and mutilate files as you wish. Now let's unlock the power of ed with regular expressions.

Chapter 101: Regular Expressions and Searches

A regular expression, or *regex*, is a string that defines a pattern of text. It's most commonly a string of text meant to match another string of text. Ed can scan its buffer for text that matches the regular expression, either pointing it out for your consideration or performing automatic transformations on everything that matches the pattern. Regular expressions are used most commonly for searches and text replacement. Ed's regular expressions helped inspire later regex standards, such as POSIX. As the originator, though, ed does not trouble itself to support all the bloat of POSIX. These days, ed regular expressions are called "basic regular expressions." You will find impure ed versions that have been distended by other regex versions but again, those are for the weak of mind and unworthy of our attention. Despite their reputation, looking at regular expressions does not cause incurable madness—that's "extended" regexes you're thinking of.

Before you can use any of ed's amazing search and transformation features, you'll need to understand how to create regular expressions.

Regular Expression Format

Regular expressions commonly (but not always) appear between slashes. Ed's documentation uses re as the sample regular expression, which would be shown as `/re/`. Between those slashes you'll see characters, wildcards, character classes, escaped characters, and modifiers.

35

Any single *character* matches itself. If you wanted to match the letters "t," "h," and "e," in that order, you'd use a regex like `/the/`.

Regexes use the period (`.`) as a *wildcard*. It matches any character.

A *character class* appears in square brackets (`[]`). A class describes a bunch of characters that can appear in the expression. We'll cover those in detail in "Character Classes" later this chapter.

An *escaped character* lets you include a character that has a special purpose within the regex. The most obvious example is if you need to include a slash in your regex. The slash is used to delimit a regex, so you can't do `///`. You need to use a backslash (`\`) as an escape character, to tell ed that the character should be treated literally rather than as part of the expression. An escaped backslash would look like `\/`, and a regex to match a slash would become `/\//`. Searching for a period requires `\.`, while a square bracket needs `\[` or `\]`. Escaping can also transform a regular character into a special character, such as the braces used for counts and the parentheses needed by backreferences. When do you use which? It all makes perfect sense if you read the source code, but right now just nod and smile and follow the examples.

Modifiers change how the regular expression gets interpreted. Suffixes are the most common regular expression modifiers, and appear after the final slash. Many of these modifiers are exactly like commands—for example, `p` tells the regex to print the match, while `n` prints the match and adds the line number.

Let's see how regular expressions work with a few highly artificial examples.

Searching in Ed

All too often you know you used a word in a document, but you're not certain where it was. There's no need to print out the whole file; ed lets you search for words by regular expression. Take this list of words— many similar, some not, printed with addresses so we can more easily discuss them.

```
*,n
1        the
2        their
3        then
4        Them
5        there
6        they're
7        thereafter
8        2
9        3weasels
10       4 theremin
11       /the/
12       pet rats
13       [pedicular]
14       hamster5
```

Entering your regex as a command, slashes and all, tells ed to search for the next line containing text that matches the regex. I warned you this was artificial, so let's search for the regex /the/.

```
*/the/
the
*.=
1
*
```

The first line of the buffer matches. The search command set our address to the matching line. To search forward for the same regex, enter a double slash.

```
*//
their
```

Okay, that's line 2. I could keep asking for the address, or I could add a command after the search command. Remember the n command that adds line numbers? It works as a search modifier.

```
*//n
3          then
*//n
5          there
```

Hang on—what happened to line 4? Looking at the file, the word "Them" includes the. Shouldn't that match? No, it shouldn't. "Them" begins with a capital letter. The regex matches only a literal, lower case, the. You'll need to use a character class to make the search case-insensitive.

Walking through a buffer one line at a time gets tedious, though. Use the g command in front of the search term to search for a regex globally, on the entire buffer. Put your regex right after the g. To print all the matches, add the trailing p command as a modifier.

Here I globally search for the string "re," or the regex /re/, and print the results.

```
*g/re/p
there
they're
thereafter
4 theremin
```

The p command is the default action of a search, so you could skip it. Searches print their results automatically unless you say otherwise. But then this example wouldn't illustrate where the newcomer grep(1) command came from, would it? If you wanted to print line numbers while searching for "re," though, use the n command instead of p.

```
*g/re/n
5          there
6          they're
7          thereafter
10         4 theremin
```

Yes, grep has a command line flag to print line numbers—but why would you bother looking up that flag, when it's conveniently built right into ed?[6]

When you do a global search, your address is set to the last match.

Search a subset of the buffer by putting addresses before the g command.

```
*1,10g/re/n
```

To search backwards from the current address, use question marks instead of slashes around the regex.

```
*10
4 theremin
*?re?n
7        thereafter
```

The previous match is address 7. To repeat the current backward search, enter two question marks.

```
*??n
6        they're
```

The // and ?? commands both refer to the most recent regex, allowing you to move forward and backwards on the current search.

Running Commands on Searches

Commands to print the matching lines aren't the only things you can do with searches. You can give the search any command other than a search command (g, G, v, or v).

An easy example is deleting matches. The d command deletes the current address. Here I strip away all lines that match the string "re."

```
*g/re/d
```

Your buffer just shrank. If you're following along at home, undo this before the next example.

---

6   What Unix really needs is a gren(1) command. Because grep(1) gets lonely.

Say you want to move lines that match the regular expression to the end of the buffer. Use the m command, with the $ destination address that matches the end of the file.

*g/re/m$

What does this give us?

*,n

```
1        the
2        their
3        then
4        Them
5        2
6        3weasels
7        /the/
8        pet rats
9        [pedicular]
10       hamster5
11       there
12       they're
13       thereafter
14       4 theremin
```

Ed moved through the buffer. Every time it found a match, it moved that line to the end of the file. You just automatically re-ordered your buffer! Doing so with a simple regex like this looks trivial, but when you build more complicated regexes you'll find it useful.

Suppose you wanted to move everything that matches to the beginning of the file. The command differs by only the destination address, but the results look far different.

```
*g/re/m0
*,n
1          4 theremin
2          thereafter
3          they're
4          there
5          the
6          their
7          then
8          Them
9          2
10         3weasels
11         /the/
14         hamster5
```

The words that match our regular expression are at the top of the file, but their ordering has reversed. What was line 11 is now line 1, line 10 is now 2, and so on. In doing the global search, ed processes each line in order. Lines matching the regex get moved up to address zero. Line 5 matched, and got moved to zero. Line 6 then matched, and got moved to zero. Moving lines to the top of the stack—er, buffer—one at a time reverses their order. The same thing happens if you move lines to any address other than $, such as an address in the middle of the file.

Avoiding this reversal requires interactive editing with a regex.

Interactive Searching

Sometimes you must perform specific actions on every matching line. Rather than forcing you to run a search and then a separate command on each line, ed can pause after each match and give you a chance to run a command. Use the G command to tell ed to pause after each match.

```
*G/re/n
5          there
```

I can hit ENTER to continue, or type a command. I'm going to use the m command to move this line to address 0, or the beginning of the file.

```
m0
```

Ed proceeds to show me the next match. I move each to a successive address at the beginning of the file.

```
6          they're
m1
7          thereafter
m2
10         4 theremin
m3
```

At the end of the search, ed displays the current address and the contents of that address.

```
4          4 theremin
*
```

What have I done here? I've moved every match to the beginning of the buffer, but retained the original ordering.

```
*,n
1          there
2          they're
3          thereafter
4          4 theremin
5          the
6          their
7          then
8          Them
9          2
10         3weasels
11         /the/
12         pet rats
13         [pedicular]
14         hamster5
```

If you screw up this kind of operation, ed considers searches a single operation. You can undo even a complicated interactive search with u.

Inverted Matches

If you want the search to hit on everything that doesn't match your regex, use the v command. Here I display numbered lines of everything that doesn't match "the."

```
*v/the/n
4          Them
8          2
9          3weasels
12         pet rats
13         [pedicular]
14         hamster5
```

Again, "Them" doesn't match "the"—searches are case-sensitive.

To interactively edit each non-matching line use the v command. This works exactly like interactive editing of matches with G.

Character Classes

Being able to match a string is fine, but any lowly WYSIWYG text editor can do that. What gives regular expressions power is their ability to describe types of text to match on. You want to match alphanumeric strings? Regex can do that. You want to hit any line that contains the numbers 3 through 5? No problem. All of these and more are built on character classes.

A character class is a list of matching characters in square brackets. The class [Tt] matches either a lower-case or upper-case letter T, while [Hh] matches either type of H. One appearance of a character class matches a single character in the regex. Character classes let us perform case-insensitive searches.

```
*g/[Tt][Hh][Ee]/n
1          the
2          their
3          then
4          Them
...
```

43

Unlike searching on plain old /the/, this search picks up line 4 with its leading capital T.

You can also list ranges of characters, separated by hyphens. The class [a-z] matches every lower-case letter, while [A-Z] matches upper case letters and [0-9] matches all digits. You can have multiple ranges in a single class, such as [a-zA-Z0-9]. If you need a class to include the hyphen put it first. The class [-/[]] matches a hyphen, a slash, and either square bracket, while [/-[]] matches whatever your system says the characters from / to [are, as well as].

Ranges can contain any characters you like. If I need to match lines containing the letters a through d, as well as u through z, lower case, my class would be [a-du-z].

*g/[a-du-z]/n
```
6         they're
7         thereafter
9         3weasels
12        pet rats
13        [pedicular]
14        gelato5
```

Use such classes to narrow in on exactly what you want, and an anchor to say where you want it.

Anchors

An anchor attaches a regex to a position in the line. They let you perform searches like "has a digit at the beginning of the line" or "ends with a Z." A caret (^) anchors the regex to the front of the line, while the dollar sign ($) anchors it to the end. Here I search for all lines that start with the letter "t."

*g/^t/n
```
1         the
2         their
3         then
5         there
6         they're
7         thereafter
```

Similarly, you could search for every line that ends in a number.

```
*g/[0-9]$/n
8        2
```

Anchors help you narrow down your searches.

Inverted Classes

Inverted classes contain all characters except those listed in the class. The first character in an inverted class must be a caret (^). A class like [^w] means "All characters except a lower case w."

Searching based on inverse character classes quickly gets really tricky. If you want to use inverse classes, make your classes very short and simple. To search for everything that doesn't include a character class, you're much better off using the v or v command. This search excludes everything that includes an upper case character.

```
*v/[A-Z]/n
```

Inverted classes are most useful inside a more complex regex. Suppose I want to match everything containing the letter "e," so long as the character following it isn't "t."

```
*g/e[^t]/n
2        their
3        Them
4        then
...
```

If you've been paying attention you'll notice that our first line, *the*, is missing. This contains the letter e, and it's not followed by a letter t. Why doesn't it show up? The regex says we're looking for the letter "e" followed by any character other than "t." There's no character following the "e" in *the*, so it doesn't match.

Note the difference in caret placement between the inverted class and the anchor. The inverted class uses a caret inside square brackets, while the anchor goes outside any square brackets. This lets you perform searches like listing all the lines that start with a character other than "t."

```
*g/^[^t]/n
4          Them
8          2
9          3weasels
10         4 theremin
11         /the/
12         pet rats
13         [pedicular]
14         gelato5
```

You're probably better off using a command like v/^t/n, however. Regular expressions are tricky. Inverted classes are doubly tricky. Avoid them if you can.

Multiple Matches and Wildcards

Sometimes you'll want to match more than one of a character, or perhaps even zero or more of a character. Ed provides operators for this.

Use the curly braces to match a character a certain number of times. Put the count directly after the character you want to match. A regex like e{2} would tell ed to match two "e" characters in a row. (You could also use a regex like ee, but that wouldn't let me set up the more complicated regexes we're about to see.) Normally, ed treats curly braces in a regex as characters to match. Escaping the braces tells ed to treat them special. This makes your expression a little more complicated.

```
*g/e\{2\}/n
15         thee
16         theee
17         theeeeee
18         theeeeeen
```

We get four matches.[7] Hang on a minute—there's way more than two es in a row in lines 16, 17, and 18. What happened? This just demonstrates that ed is more detail-oriented than you are. Line 16 has two pairs of *es* in a row, with the middle e shared between them. Lines 17 and 18 have three e-pairs in a row, plus more when you count the shared *es*.

Matching a specific set of characters demands careful thought. What, exactly, do you want to match? I want to match two letters, exactly two letters, with something other than an "e" after them. Try using a character class that excludes e.

```
*g/e\{2\}[^e]/n
18      theeeeeen
```

That's definitely two *es* in a row, followed by a character that isn't an e.

Or suppose I want two *es* in a row after a character other than *e*, and to attach those *es* to the end of the line.

```
*g/[^e]e\{2\}$/n
15      thee
```

Matching identical characters in a row demands you think carefully.

Basic regular expressions let you match a range of characters. If you want to match, say, two to five *es* in a row, this looks like what you'd want. Express this by giving the lower limit, a comma, and the upper limit, such as `e{2,5}`. You'll need to escape the braces in the actual ed command.

---

7   These words didn't show up in our list before? Weird. It's almost like the author needed multiple identical letters in a row for this section, but didn't bother to go back and update any of the earlier examples.

```
*g/e\{2,5\}/n
15        thee
16        theee
17        theeeee
18        theeeeeen
```

This hits the same problem as looking for two in a row. You'll need to add other characteristics to this regex to get the desired result.

```
*g/e\{2,5\}$/n
15        thee
16        theee
17        theeeeee
```

This might look good at first glance, but if you count closely you'll see that line 17 has six *e*s in a row. We need to set a boundary before it, using the not-*e* class.

```
*g/[^e]e\{2,5\}$/n
15        thee
16        theee
```

If you want to match anything that has a given number of characters or more, give the comma without an upper limit, as in {2, }.

```
*g/e\{2,\}/p
thee
theee
theeeeee
theeeeeen
```

In certain cases you'll want *zero* or more of a character. Indicate zero or more with an asterisk (*). To get really crazy, combine this with the wildcard . that represents any character.

```
*g/.*/n
1         the
2         their
...
```

Yes, this matches every line in our file. Pretty useless, no?

The wildcard and asterisk are not useful on their own, but combined with other characters, classes, and anchors they become extremely powerful. Suppose you want to find all lines that start with a letter but end with a number. We've used regexes like `^[a-zA-Z]` to find letters at the front of a line. A regex like `[0-9]$` will find numbers at the end, no problem. But combining them gets tricky... until we allow other characters in the middle.

```
*g/^[a-zA-Z].*[0-9]$/n
14        gelato5
```

This allows you to declare you don't care what's in the middle or how long the string is. If it starts with a letter and ends with a number, you get it. The period represents zero or more of something, and the asterisk matches any character, so we're allowing zero or more of anything else. This lets us match really short strings like "a1" without excluding longer strings.

The asterisk can cause some counterintuitive output for folks accustomed to shell programming. You might expect a regex like `*g/ther*/n` to show words beginning with "ther," but you'd be wrong

```
*g/ther*/n
1         the
2         their
3         then
...
```

The asterisk matches zero or more "r" characters at the en
expression. The string "the" has zero "r" characters, so it mat
you want one or more "r" characters, say so with a regex lik

Commands and Searches

One powerful feature of searches and regular expressions is that you can run commands after a search. Suppose you want to duplicate every line that matches a regular expression. As you'll be changing the file, start with a plain search to be sure your regex matches the stuff you think it'll match.

```
*g/there/n
5          there
7          thereafter
10         4 theremin
```

That looks right. Now use the t command to copy the line, but use 'estination address of ".".—the current line. This will insert the copy after the current line.[8] Add the n command to print the affected

```
ョ/t. n
there
hereafter
theremin
```

ine numbers. We've duplicated the matching lines on
's.

is most useful combined with substitutions, which

d of t
ches.
e rr*.

8
h
or

ı *Star Trek*. You can't make its
–—it duplicates each line only

Chapter 110: Substitution

While regular expressions let you search and manipulate matching lines, ed lets you change text based on those same regular expressions. Regex-based *substitution* is an incredibly powerful search and replace function that lesser text editors can only dream of. While clumsy regexes can shred your buffer, with practice you can quickly and easily transform your text.

I've been swearing at—er, working with—regular expressions for decades. Even today, I do a search with a regular expression before performing a substitution based on that regex. Regular expressions are subtle and quick to anger. Always test them first. Even once I think they work, I keep a copy of the untransformed data.

Use the s command for a substitution, followed by the regular expression and the new text. Separate each piece with a slash.

```
s/regex/new/
```

We'll start with a simple substitution—but to achieve that, we'll start with a simple search. Using the same list of words as Chapter 101, suppose we want to change all instances of "there" to "then." First, search for your regular expression to see if you get what you think you're going to get.

```
*g/there/n
5          there
7          thereafter
10         4 theremin
```

Three matches. The search set our address to the last match, so let's go back up to the top of the file and try a substitution.

```
*1
the
*s/there/then/
?
no match
```

An error? But our search saw matching strings in the buffer! Remember, ed works on a line-by-line basis. Line 1 doesn't match our regex, so it errors. You must use a search (either manual or automatic) to target substitutions.

Substitutions allow you to programmatically correct errors. Consider one of the entries on our word list.

```
*18
theeeeeen
```

"Theeeeeen" is not a word. The e key obviously stuck when someone typed "then." We can use a substitution to fix it. Here, I replace any string of two or more *e*s with a single e.

```
*s/e\{2,\}/e/
```

Check the line now.

```
*18
then
```

If I knew ahead of time I wanted to print the result, I could have added the p command at the end of the substitution. We'll cover the few specific commands that work at the end of a substitution.

```
*s/e\{2,\}/e/p
```

If escaping all of those braces gives you trouble, you could choose the simpler option of repeating the substitution. The s command repeats the previous substitution.

```
*s/ee/e/p
theeeeen
*s
theeeen
*s
theeen
*s
theen
*s
then
*s
?
no match
```

You might notice that that the substitution only affects one match. Consider a line like this.

```
*19
wXXhXXaXXtXX XXisXX this?XX
```

I don't know how all those XX chunks got in there, but they need to go. You might try a substituting one of these strings with nothing.

```
*s/XX//p
whXXaXXtXX XXisXX this?XX
```

The substitution engine does the least amount of work you require of it.[9] It matches the first XX, between the w and the h, and yanks it out. You could tell it which of the matches to pull out by giving a number as an argument. Here, I substitute nothing for the seventh XX.

```
*s/XX//7p
wXXhXXaXXtXX XXisXX this?
```

---

9   Substitutions are suspiciously human in that regard.

It's useful to make minor tweaks to an existing line. The problem with such substitutions is that you have to count. It also makes repeating the substitution less useful. To repeat the last substitution, hit s again.

```
*s/XX//p
whXXaXXtXX XXisXX this?XX
*s
whaXXtXX XXisXX this?XX
…
*s
what is this?
```

I could add a number after the s to repeat the substitution only on a specific match on the line.

Eliminating all the matches is much simpler with the g (global) modifier. It tells ed to perform the substitution on every match it finds on the current line. I'll also add the p modifier to print the results.

```
*s/XX//gp
what is this?
```

Problem solved.

Combining Searches and Substitution

Having to find the lines that contain the text you want to substitute would suck the joy out of ed. Rather than harsh your mellow, ed can combine searches and substitution. Give your substitution after the search, to say "if this matches, perform this substitution."

Our example tries to find the word "there" and replace it with "then." The search is pretty straightforward: g/there/. Much as in the shell, a backslash means "continued on the next line." I then give the desired substitution.

```
*g/there/ \
s/there/then/
test there
thereafter
4 theremin
```

Ed prints the lines that match the search. But look at those lines now.

```
*5p
test then
*7p
thenafter
*10p
4 thenmin
```

Substitution success! Ed considers this combined search-and-substitute (or, as the kids would say, search and *replace*) a single command, so you could reverse it with u. Which I do, because this is a daft example. But you might use this in a script to update user login scripts, updating links to migrated servers, or any other tedious task. We'll see some examples in Chapter 111.

The backslash that splits this operation into two lines isn't needed. If you put it all on one line, ed doesn't show the lines that match the search.

```
*g/there/ s/there/then/
*
```

You can have multiple substitutions in one command, but each substitution must appear on separate lines, separated by a backslash.

```
*g/there/ s/there/then/\
s/t/T/n
5        Test then
7        Thenafter
10       4 Thenmin
```

This swaps out "then" for "there" and capitalizes the first T of each line.

While you can use apparently unrelated regexes inside your substitution, a failure of one substitution aborts all later substitutions. Arrange your substitutions carefully.

Now that you've seen the complicated form, let's simplify slightly. When you want to perform a substitution on the regex you're searching for, you can use the % address to perform the substitution on all available lines.

`*%s/there/Then/`

Note this isn't exactly the same as the more complicated substitution above, though; line 5 capitalizes "test" rather than "then." The full version is much more flexible, so we'll focus on that.

Subexpressions and Backreferences

A *subexpression* is a part of a regular expression. Use subexpressions to split a line into chunks, such as "everything before what we care about, what we care about, and everything after that." Subexpressions are marked in parenthesis, such as `([a-zA-Z0-9])`. Much like curly braces, you must backslash-escape parentheses to tell ed that you're using them for a subexpression. Otherwise, ed looks for literal parenthesis characters. While I'm introducing subexpressions, though, we'll skip the backslashes for clarity.

For ed to remember the whole line, the subexpression must match the whole line that contains the string you want. The period and wildcards come in useful here. While `/the/` matches a line containing the string "the," remembering the whole line requires using `/.*the.*/` —zero or more of something, what we really want, and then zero or more of something. Enclose the regex in parenthesis to have ed remember it as a subexpression: `/(.*the.*)/`.

A *backreference* lets you refer to the literal text matched by a subexpression. You can use backreferences within searches, but they overwhelmingly appear in substitutions. Ed recalls subexpressions by the order you define them in. Your first subexpression is backreference one, the second backreference two, and so on. Indicate a backreference with a backslash and its number, such as \1, \2, and so on.

Our sample regex, /(.*the.*)/, tells ed to remember one subexpression. There's only a single backreference, \1.

How would you use a subexpression and a backreference? You might want to search for every line that includes opening and closing quote marks. Human beings are notoriously inconsistent, so those strings might use either single or double quotes. I define a character class with both sorts of quotes, ['"]. Put that class inside parentheses to declare it a subexpression: (['"]). We could have any number of characters after that, up until the next appearance of whatever character matched the subexpression: .*. Whatever character we found in the subexpression is our first backreference, or \1. Put it all together into the regex (['"]).*\1. I want to use this in a search command, so I'll need to backslash-escape the parenthesis to tell ed this is a subexpression: \(['"]\).*\1. Use the g command to print the lines matching this regex.

```
*g/\(['"]\).*\1/
"bleeeeep"
unconscious 'people'
```

Backreferences work with substitutions. Here I want to prefix every line that includes "the" with the string "HIT-." For your edification, I add the p command to print the results. I use a g command to target lines that match the regex /the/, so the substitution only happens on lines that contain that regex. The actual substitution uses a subexpression to capture the entire line, then a backreference to place that captured string in the regex.

```
*g/the/\
s/\(.*\)/HIT-\1/p
the
HIT-the
their
HIT-their
...
```

The first line performs a search on our target regex, selecting lines that include "the." The command is broken into two lines, so ed prints the matching lines. The second line does the substitution, adding the string HIT- and then adding the \1 backreference to recall the first and only subexpression. I added the trailing p to print the results after the substitution, showing before and after. Each matching string has the desired prefix.

Suppose you want a case-insensitive match on "the," and you not only want to remember what you matched, you want to subdivide that memory into before, matching, and after chunks. Each piece needs its own parenthesis, giving you something like /(.*)([tT][hH][eE])(.*)/.

This regex has three subexpressions, so you'll backreference them as \1, \2, and \3.

How would you use this? Maybe you want to put "HERE->" and "<-HERE" around the match.[10] Your substitution will need the first subexpression, then add a HERE->, the second subexpression, a <-HERE, and the last subexpression.

The first line, the search, aims our substitution only at lines matching a case-insensitive "the." The second line uses a regex with subexpressions to break that line into pieces, then performs a substitution with backreferences to glue the line together. Using this requires escaping all these parenthesis with backslashes, demonstrating why I skipped the backslashes while creating the regex.

---

10   This is traditionally called "regex debugging."

```
*g/[tT][hH][eE]/\
s/\(.*\)\([tT][hH][eE]\)\(.*\)/\1HERE->\2<-HERE\3/p
the
HERE->the<-HERE
their
HERE->the<-HEREir
then
HERE->the<-HEREn
Them
HERE->The<-HEREm
...
```

You can now see where your regex matched on each line, as well as the rest of the line.

This particular substitution could be simplified with the % address, giving us:

```
% s/\(.*\)\([tT][hH][eE]\)\(.*\)/\1HERE->\2<-HERE\3/p.
```

But that wouldn't let us use multiple substitutions in a single search.

Multiple Substitutions

You used a regex search to target your substitutions, but that doesn't mean you must use that regex in your substitution. Ed lets you stack multiple substitutions after a search, permitting complicated data transformations in a single command.

Go back to Chapter 101 for a moment, where we tried to match strings containing two to five *es* in a row. That turns out to be difficult, because regexes can match multiple entries in one line. A string of six *es* is only two groups of three *es*, after all. Realistically, though, we'd perform that search because we want to transform that data in some way. Stacking substitutions after a search can let you perform myriad transformations without the weakness of resorting to young whippersnapper tools like sed(1).

I have a text file containing occasional corrupt data. Words should contain either two or fewer *es* in a row, or greater than five. If a word contains strings of three, four, or five *es* in a row, those strings should be replaced with two *es*. If it has one, two, or six or more *es* in a row, I want to leave it alone.

This takes careful thinking about our regular expressions. Identifying strings with a limited range of characters requires identifying what's on each side of the characters of interest. There's basically three options: the *es* can be at the beginning or end of the word, or they can be in the middle. We'll need a regex and substitution for all three cases. Again, as we discuss the regexes I'll skip the backslash escapes for clarity. They'll go into the ed command line.

For the first case, where the string of *es* are at the end of the line, use the not-e class (`[^e]`) to identify the beginning of the e-string. Then add the regex for three to five *es*: `e{3,5}`. Anchor the regex to the end of the line with `$`. That gives us a substitution regex of `[^e]e{3,5}$`. We want to replace this with whatever the not-e class matches, plus two *es*. Remembering what the not-e class matched requires a subexpression, so add the parenthesis around `[^e]` to create `([^e])e{3,5}$`. We replace this mess with the backreference and two es, or `\1ee`. The final substitution statement looks like `s/([^e])e{3,5}$/\1ee/`.

If the string of *es* are at the beginning of the line, we basically reverse the end-of-line regex. Use the caret (`^`) to anchor the regex to the front of the line. Add the `e{3,5}` regex for three to five *es* right after the caret, and use the not-e class in a subexpression: `([^e])`. That gives us a regex of `^e{3,5}([^e])`. We want to replace this with two *es*, plus whatever the not-e subexpression matched, giving us `ee\1`. The final substitution statement looks like `s/^e{3,5}([^e])/ee\1/`.

Having a string of *es* in the middle of the line steals elements from both of the previous regexes. We need subexpressions for not-e before and after the string of *es*, with the three-to-five *es* in the middle. That gives us `([^e])e{3,5}([^e])`. With two subexpressions we need two backreferences in the substitution, or `\1ee\2`. The final substitution statement looks like `s/([^e])e{3,5}([^e])/\1ee\2/`.

Aim these substitutions with a search command. The substitutions have no effect on strings of *es* longer than five characters, so we can run them on any pattern of three or more *es*: `e{3,}`. Our combined search-and-substitution command will look something like this—again, with backslash escapes omitted for clarity.

```
g/e{3,}/ \
s/([^e])e{3,5}$/\1ee/p\
s/^e{3,5}([^e])/ee\1/p\
s/([^e])e{3,5}([^e])/\1ee\2/p
```

I added the `p` (print) command to each of the substitutions, so that we can see which substitution triggers what change in each line. It's classic printf-style debugging. As we used a backslash to separate the initial search and the first regex, ed will print the matching term. Each match produces four lines of output: the original line, the line after an e-in-front substitution, the line after the e-in-back substitution, and the line after the e-in-the-middle substitution.

Adding the backslash-escapes in and running the command produces output much like so.

```
*  g/e\{3,\}/ \
s/\([^e]\)e\{3,5\}$/\1ee/p\
s/^e\{3,5\}\([^e]\)/ee\1/p\
s/\([^e]\)e\{3,5\}\([^e]\)/\1ee\2/p
theee
thee
thee
thee
```

Our first match has three es at the end. The first substitution catches and shortens it.

```
theeeeee
theeeeee
theeeeee
theeeeee
```

The search catches a word with six consecutive es. None of the substitution regexes matched it, so it escapes unscathed.

```
eeeeek!!!
eeeeek!!!
eek!!!
eek!!!
```

Here's a line beginning with five es. It gets whacked by substitution number two.

```
bleeeeep
bleeeeep
bleeeeep
bleep
```

Unless you have a really long string of obscenities, two *es* is enough to bleep something out. The last substitution regex catches and trims it.

All of this works beautifully, until someone points out that your regexes didn't include the special case of a line containing only three to five *es*. You'll add this substitution statement and rerun the command, exactly as you would with any other tool. We all have these moments. To perform complex multi-regex substitutions like this you're best off doing it in scripts, as discussed in Chapter 111.

Underlining via Substitution

The examples we've demonstrated have all been pretty simple. Let's use them to build something more substantial. We'll use substitution and plain text to underline every line that contains our regex.[11] Yes, plain text doesn't support underlining, but we're going to do it anyway, just the way Real Sysadmins did back in the day.

We'll develop this iteratively, starting with the simple regex "the." Once we have a working proof of concept, we'll expand it.

Our file contains a bunch of lines like this (shown with addresses).

```
1       the
2       but then
3       their
4       Them
5       4 theremin
6       thebadgerthe
7       thee
```

Start by duplicating lines that match our regex, copying them in-place.

*g/the/t.

This gives us a buffer containing a bunch of duplicate lines.

```
1       the
2       the
3       but then
4       but then
5       their
6       their
...
```

Remember that the t (transfer, or copy) command sets your address to that of the copied line. Each time this search hits a match, ed sets our address to the copied line. If you perform a substitution immediately after doing the copy, the substitution affects only the current line—the copy. To underline lines that match our regex, transform every character in a matching line to an equals sign.

---

11   Because even Primordial Sysadmins had management that wanted pretty reports.

```
*g/the/t. \
s/./=/g
*,n
1          the
2          ===
3          but then
4          =====
5          their
6          ====
7          Them
8          there
9          =====
```

Lines that match "the" get a proper ASCII underline as Thompson and Ritchie intended, while non-matching lines do not.

Partial Underlining

Underlining is useful, but maybe you don't want to underline the whole line, though. Perhaps you want to only underline the part of the line that matches the regex. That's not much harder to do. We'll start with the underlining command and modify it.

We need to break up the copied line into stuff that will become blank space and stuff that will become underlining. While there's many ways to handle this problem, my approach splits the line with a newline amidst the substitution. I removed the escape backslashes for clarity, because the remaining backslashes are important.

```
s/(.*)(the).*/x\1\
\2/
```

The regex part of the substitution includes two subexpressions. One is everything before our desired regex (.*). The second is the regex itself, (the). The regex has a third piece, .*, for everything else. The third piece is not a subexpression, so ed won't bother to remember it. (Strictly speaking the third part isn't necessary, but I find it easier to explicitly say "there might be stuff after this" when reading my own code days or years later.)

64

Now consider the substitution part. If the search term appears first, we'd have a blank first backreference. Later parts of this command assume we have something here, so we put a letter x at the beginning of the line no matter what. We have a backreference for the first part and jump to a newline. The newline isn't a "command continues on next line" statement; instead, it gets inserted into our substitution. Ed can tell the difference because the newline appears in the middle of a substitution. We're splitting the line into two lines.

On the next line, the second backreference brings in the text we searched for. Combined with the earlier search, our buffer becomes something like this.

```
1       the
2       x
3       the
4       but then
5       xbut
6       then
...
```

Everything that matches our regex gets busted up into groups of three lines. The first line in each group is the original line. The second is a copy of everything before the regex match, with an "x" prepended. The third is the string that matches the regex. Everything after the regex match is discarded.

In our first group of three, line 2 contains only an "x" because there's nothing before the regex match. Line 3 contains what matched our regex.

In the second group of three (lines 4-6), line 5 shows what appeared before the regex match, but with a prepended "x." Line 6 shows the regex match.

After each substitution, our address is set to the last line of the three. That's the snipped-off chunk of text that matches our regex. Transform each of those characters into an equals sign with the really simple substitution `s/./=/g`. We need the trailing `g` command so that every match gets transformed into an equals sign, not just the first one. This transforms our text like so.

```
1          the
2          x
3          ===
4          but then
5          xbut
6          ===
...
```

There's our equal-sign underlines, but they need appropriate spacing to put them under our terms. That's why we saved the "stuff before the regex" lumps, the second line of each three-line group. Use relative addressing—the leading minus sign—to perform a substitution on the *previous* line, replacing every character with a space, as in: `-s/./ /g`. Working on a line changes our address to that line. This creates lines like so.

```
1          the
2
3          ===
4          but then
5
6          ===
...
```

The second line of each triplet looks empty, but contains blank spaces. Every line has at least one space in it, from the "x" used as a placeholder. That's an extra character that will mess up our formatting, so use `s/^ //\` to remove it. There won't be any visible difference, but our next command will now work.

The `j` (join) command defaults to connecting the following line to the end of the current line. The blank characters provide the spaces to have the equals-sign underlines line up.

All together now! Add in the necessary backslash escapes before each of the parentheses and curly braces, and we can underline "the" on each line.

```
*  g/the/t.\
s/\(.*\)\(the\).*/x\1\
\2/\
s/./=/g\
-s/./ /g\
s/^ //\
j
*,p
the
===
but then
    ===
their
===
Them
4 theremin
  ===
thebadgerthe
         ===
thee
===
```

See? Microsoft Word has nothing on ed. *NOTHING.*

Shortcuts and Alternates

Ed is smart enough that it doesn't need to you to spell absolutely everything out. Consider the format of a search.

```
g/regex/commands
```

The final slash is there to separate the regex from any commands. If you're not running any extra commands, that last slash is unnecessary. You can drop it.

```
*g/gela
gelato
```

In modern (mid-1980s and later) versions of ed, you don't even need the g command. A slash on its own triggers a search.

```
*/\[.*icu
[pedicular]
```

67

Similarly, the final slash on a substitution separates the substitution from any trailing commands. If you don't have any trailing commands, you can ditch that final slash.

```
*s/vim/ed
ed
```

If you want to replace the regex with nothing, as in `s/regex//`, you can shorten even further. Ed knows you want to do a substitution, because you used the s command. You've given it the regex and no substitution, so it just does it for you. This makes pulling surplus words out of a document easy.

```
*s/emacs
```

Searches and substitutions have a truly amazing number of backslashes. If you write a regex that looks for slashes, it starts to resemble the jaw of a Tyrannosaurus. Ed eases this problem by supporting *alternate delimiters*. When you use the s or g command, whatever character appears next takes the place of the slash. Here I want to search for slashes, so I use the letter "m" as an alternate delimiter.

```
*gm/
/the/
```

Alternate delimiters also work in substitutions. Here I use "@" as a delimiter.

```
*s@nano@heresy
```

Next I delete the first "h" from the current line, using "m" as a delimiter.

```
*smh
```

Making commands short is the Unix way. Alternate delimiters improve your ability to shorten commands.

You now have a good grasp on how to use ed interactively. Before you go, though, let's look at reusing ed commands through scripts.

Chapter 111: Scripting

Scripting is an utterly essential component of systems administration. Using ed in your scripts will not only simplify certain tasks, it will demonstrate your moral superiority over the lesser so-called sysadmins surrounding you.

Consider our command to underline a regular expression on each line, from the last chapter. You really don't want to type all that every time you need to perform this transformation, do you? A reusable, editable script is much better.

The key to scripting is to remember that ed is a command-driven line editor. Unlike lesser editors, it accepts instructions from standard input. It has no need to differentiate between human and script input. You can't include comments within your ed script, but you have a whole variety of ways to run your scripted ed.

The Ed Command File

The easiest way to script with ed is to create a file containing all the ed commands to run. and then just run it like so.

```
$ ed textfile < ed-commands.ed
```

The commands file contains only the ed commands you want to run.

As when you're learning any scripting method, start simple. Let's create a script to duplicate every line that matches a regex. Open your editor and follow along.

```
$ ed dup.ed
dup.ed: No such file or directory
P
*H
cannot open input file
*a
g/the/t.
,p
Q
.
*wq
14
$
```

We open an ed session and turn on prompts and detailed error messages. While ed doesn't care that the file doesn't exist, enabling verbose errors commands it to remind us about the existing error. We then append to the buffer. The first command in the script is our friend g/the/t., straight from the last chapter.

Once that search and copy finishes, the ,p command prints the file from beginning to end.

The final command in our script file is Q, to immediately quit without saving.

The dot takes us back to our editing session's command line, letting us wq to save and quit.

```
$ ed textfile < dup.ed
179
the
the
pony
their
their
...
```

The first line of output is the number of bytes in the text file, just as if you were editing the text file interactively. We then see each line of the buffer, allowing us to verify that the command file does what we thought it did.

If you're happy with the results, edit the command file so that it will save the processed file.

```
$ ed dup.ed
14
P
*H
*,n
1          g/the/t.
2          ,p
3          Q
```

Consider the necessary changes. On line 3 you no longer want to quit unconditionally; rather, it's time to save and quit. You also don't need to view the results of the transformation, so line two can get deleted. Start editing at the bottom, so that your line numbers remain consistent with the earlier printout as long as possible.

```
*3s/Q/wq
wq
```

That replaces the Q with wq. Ed displays the modified line. I could have also used the c (change) command, but a little regex practice never hurt anyone. Now kill line two, save, and quit.

```
*2d
*wq
12
```

Let's see what the script shows now.

```
$ ed textfile < dup.ed
179
266
$
```

Ed read 176 bytes and wrote 266. Your text file has been changed—and best of all, by editing with ed, there's no possibility that a slipped arrow key would mess up the command that performed the transformation. All you changed was the save routine.

If you want to hide the bytes read and written, use ed's -s flag.

You want something more complicated? A command file that underlines the last match of a regex on a line, as we did in Chapter 110, has one minor difference between the commands in the last chapter and what you need for a command script. See if you can spot it.

```
g/the/t.\
s/\(.*\)\(the\).*/x\1\
\2/\
s/./=/g\
-s/./ /g\
s/^ //\
j
wq
```

What's the difference? A script should automatically save its work, so I added wq.

Adopting ed for routine use prevents many errors only possible in so-called "visual" editors.

Ed in Shell Scripts

While command files are fine for one-off jobs, sometimes you want to integrate ed into a more complicated workflow. While you could write a shell script that calls your command file, there's no reason not to integrate those commands into the script.

Suppose you have a whole bunch of web sites running Wordpress. (I know that you wouldn't serve *your* content in such an unseemly way, but most of your customers probably can't handle wholesome, elegant technologies like Usenet.) You need to deploy an application firewall like Wordfence across the whole lot of them. Wordfence requires changes to each site's .htaccess file. You could make a whole bunch of error-prone manual edits, or use ed to systematically and reliably make those edits for you.

First, have the script find all of the files you need to change.

```
#!/bin/sh

for x in /var/www/*/.htaccess
do
```

Now use an echo statement to provide ed commands. Just to be sure, I set an address before inserting my new content before line 1.

```
    echo "1
i
# Wordfence WAF
<Files ".user.ini">
<IfModule mod_authz_core.c>
        Require all denied
</IfModule>
<IfModule !mod_authz_core.c>
        Order deny,allow
        Deny from all
</IfModule>
</Files>

# END Wordfence WAF
.
w
q" | ed $x
    done
```

At the very end, I call ed on the target file and send the contents of my echo statement into the command.

That's it. We're done!

You could use a "here" document instead, if you fear pedants whose sole reason for living is to shriek about unnecessary uses of cat(1) and echo(1). At least use an EOE (End of Ed) marker, though.

```
ed $x <<EOE
1
i
# Wordfence WAF
<Files ".user.ini">
<IfModule mod_authz_core.c>
Require all denied
</IfModule>
<IfModule !mod_authz_core.c>
Order deny,allow
Deny from all
</IfModule>
</Files>
# END Wordfence WAF
.
w
q
EOE
```

If you've come this far, you now know more about ed than almost anyone who passes themselves off as a so-called sysadmin. Practice your ed. Develop skills.

And the next time you're at a job interview where you need to demonstrate your skills by sharing your screen, establish your dominance early. Use ed.

Afterword

Okay, come on Lucas, you're not really serious here... are you?

I am. And I'm not.

This is book 13 of my *IT Mastery* series. My lucky number needed to be a special book. The opportunity to release that book on 1 April meant that it had to be extra special. Writing a book on ed in 2018 certainly qualifies as special.

But ed is a vital part of our heritage. Ed concepts and procedures have infiltrated every part of modern UNIX. It's forty-odd years old, *and still useful*. As the last couple of chapters demonstrate, you can use ed to solve real problems and perform real work.

I've worked in more than one organization where adding software to a host meant going through a laborious change control review and security audit. No Perl or Python on your system? Too bad for you, that simple bit of automation isn't happening today. Or you can fire up ed, get that pattern-matching done, and get on with your day.

Older tools like ed, awk, and sed? They're just as powerful today as ever. Take the time to master them.

The next time someone declares themselves a rock star, respond with, "So you wrote an entire operating system on a computer without a monitor? Because that's what it takes to be a real rock star."

And remember: if it doesn't include ed in every default install, it's not Unix.

Never miss a new Lucas release!

Sign up for Michael W Lucas' mailing list.
https://mwl.io

Sponsors

If you hadn't noticed, this book is a little… different. I didn't announce the title before its release. The only publicity I did was on the Internet, under the hashtag #mwlSecretBook. Despite the secrecy I offered sponsorships at my web store at https://www.tiltedwindmillpress.com, with the following description:

This sponsorship is a complete and unmitigated scam. You won't know what the book is until everybody else knows. It's a technical book, on a technical topic. Readers will learn things, and understand parts of Unix that they probably never have…

When you find out what it is, you will either be disappointed or say WTF.

When you see the printed book, you'll be disappointed all over again.

Despite my best efforts, this description did not deter the following people. If you have a bridge to sell, you should contact these folks.

Print Sponsors

Adam Thompson

Carlin Bingham

Rogier Krieger

Phi Network Systems

Lisa Hewus Fresh

William Allaire

Niall Navin

Nicolas Bouliane

Stefan Johnson

Gary Nevills

Patrons

Where the sponsors backed this particular book, a handful of fine folks sponsor absolutely everything I write, via my Patreon (https://www.patreon.com/mwlucas).

Of those, Stefan Johnson sends me fifty dollars a month to get his name in the print edition of every book I write. You can, too.

Appendix A: Jabberwocky

By Lewis Carroll

'Twas brillig, and the slithy toves
    Did gyre and gimble in the wabe:
All mimsy were the borogoves,
    And the mome raths outgrabe.

"Beware the Jabberwock, my son!
    The jaws that bite, the claws that catch!
Beware the Jubjub bird, and shun
    The frumious Bandersnatch!"

He took his vorpal sword in hand;
    Long time the manxome foe he sought—
So rested he by the Tumtum tree
    And stood awhile in thought.

And, as in uffish thought he stood,
    The Jabberwock, with eyes of flame,
Came whiffling through the tulgey wood,
    And burbled as it came!

One, two! One, two! And through and through
    The vorpal blade went snicker-snack!
He left it dead, and with its head
    He went galumphing back.

"And hast thou slain the Jabberwock?
    Come to my arms, my beamish boy!
O frabjous day! Callooh! Callay!"
    He chortled in his joy.

'Twas brillig, and the slithy toves
    Did gyre and gimble in the wabe:
All mimsy were the borogoves,
    And the mome raths outgrabe